"In a time of renewed bigotry and demonization, Harold Recinos records and celebrates the lives of brown and Spanish-speaking Americans struggling and prevailing against the odds: 'heaven is a long walk / away from the cutting / English of these streets.' The poet's brief, cascading lines convey an equal sense of urgency and intimacy—aspects that abet the collection's key themes of dispossession, faith, and the unkillable longing for justice, progress, and true inclusion. *Wading in the River* is a devoted, impassioned, and moving book."

—Cyrus Cassells
Author of Pulitzer Prize nominee *Soul Make a Path through Shouting*

"Harold Recinos' *Wading in the River* is a tour de force into politics, philosophy, religion, race, and humanity. This collection is a balm in pandemic times when we need beauty, love, and possibilities. Professor Recinos provides much-needed bread to our hungry souls."

—Eduardo Bonilla-Silva
Author of *Racism without Racists: Color-Blind Racism and the Persistence of Racial Inequality in America*

"Against the worship, so prevalent in these violent times, of a God who establishes borders, the One who drives away our enemies in fear before us, Harold J. Recinos offers in *Wading in the River* a sounder theology, in praise of 'a God who crosses borders' and 'the One who will gather us / in the dark, give life to the dead / and wipe away tears from the faces / of the frightened.'

—H. L. Hix
Professor, MFA Poetry Faculty, Fairleigh Dickinson University

"'I am brown America,' Harold Recinos writes in 'América,' one of the gems of his newest collection, *Wading in the River*, which gathers together the range of Latinx life and experience and so much more. Rich in allusions, abounding with vision, lyric to its core, *Wading in the River* is a poetic treasure."

—John Keene
Author of *Counternarratives*

"*Wading in the River* is animated by a theopoetics of *lo cotidiano*. Rooted in our precarious and pandemic times, the poems of Harold Recinos chronicle the intensity of daily living from social and racial unrest in our cities to state-sanctioned cruelty at our southern border. He lays bare the damage done to bodies marginalized by the machinations of a dysfunctional president and reveals resistance unleashed from unexpected cyberspaces by 'TikTok teens and K-Pop fans.' Composed in barrio beats of his familiar streets en el Bronx, and with lyrical Latin@ playfulness with dos lenguas, 'a sofrito English, refried words with a taste of órale people,' Recinos calls us together 'to weep for the God who has been driven into exile!'

—Carmen Nanko-Fernández
Author of *Theologizing en Espanglish*

Wading *in the* River

Wading in the *River*

Harold J. Recinos

RESOURCE *Publications* · Eugene, Oregon

WADING IN THE RIVER

Resource Publications
An Imprint of Wipf and Stock Publishers
199 W. 8th Ave., Suite 3
Eugene, OR 97401

www.wipfandstock.com

PAPERBACK ISBN: 978-1-7252-9363-2
HARDCOVER ISBN: 978-1-7252-9362-5
EBOOK ISBN: 978-1-7252-9364-9

02/12/21

Contents

The Bells

I try to understand
the world so full of
weeping like Yeats
would say. how the
sounds come from
every shore, linger
like incense inviting
prayer and becomes
a great puddle in the
dark. my cloudy eyes
try to see beyond
the weighty flags that
fly half-mast here and
abroad looking to find
places where hopeful
bells ring.

Child

you dream in a language
many on this land simply
hate. child, I only call that
beautiful! I saw you playing
in the schoolyard and on
Sunday with your mother
in a church and even one
day walking Birmingham
Bridge to make a broken
country freer. child, reach
out your hand and touch
cold-hearted people with
your gentlest big dreams.

The Steps

in stormy times the
city stoops are places
to look for joy, public
rest stops where in the
company of others you
beat darkness into dreams
and hollering stages for
people who cry with long
tears. even in the darkness
of the night you can see
old folks leaning out the
window, winos who were
baptized in the local church
downing another pint, kids
with runny noses dashing
between parked cars and hear
soothing songs drifting down
the aging street. believe me,
time is lost on these cracked
steps where dark faces find ways
to parole laughter and heaven
on the block.

The Wait

you could see the stars
through the bedroom
window always looking
the same through the
passing years with their
limitless mysteries nearly
concealed. music drifted
in from the other room,
the sound of an airy
charanga flute, sweet
minor wails struck on
piano keys, the wistful
voice of a singer telling
night time stories about
exhausted lovers. I saw
three widows from the
same window walking
south on Mapes Avenue
resisting habits of sleep
and carrying half-finished
letters to a mailbox they
never send. my thoughts
wandered to the times I
saw them in sleep and
stood beside them on the

corner waiting and waiting
for God to show up.

Up Against Whiteness

every morning you could
find him standing with café
and a buttered roll leaning
against a wall next to the
entrance to Lincoln Hospital.
he took his first breath in it,
grew up attending the public
schools, worked in a factory
on Southern Boulevard, and
paid with hard work dues to
be called a citizen. the press
ready to print good white lies
never did say a kind word about
spics like him. you see, he was
blamed for rising crime, failing
schools, drug epidemics, economic
decline and just about anything
white politicians imagined to lay on
him. he was baptized in the basement
of a pretty church beneath a sanctuary
set aside for English speaking Christians
who thought they were free of Sin. one
summer day, he greeted the Mayor who
made a visit to the block sporting a broken
English smile. and hear this, he once stood

on the corner with grown men who shined
shoes on the boulevard and they wept like
hungry kids when they heard news that King
was killed. he believed the rejected prophet
still roamed places with poverty and battered
by hate. he once told me King was
leaning against the hospital wall with
despised Puerto Ricans and young
Black men to whisper in their precious
ears God says hate fails!

Color Blind

in your colorblind world
poetry from people like me
is called identity speech,
conceptual aesthetics or
a society linked thing. in
your colorblind ways no
one admits the United States
is a racial term given birth by
genocide, African enslavement
and the need to crush the breath
right out of us. in your colorblind
days savagery is never white,
dreams cannot be colorful and
a Lord who mumbles English has
never let a tear roll down his fair
cheeks. in your colorblind thoughts
you cannot confess our Black and
Brown faces are blessed with more
humanity than the abracadabra
color blindness you think true!

The Ringing

no one listens closely
to the cracked church
bells ringing off pitch
about the dark young
men beaten down and
the color of death that
shouts down the gospel
with brutality. no one
hears the near broken bells
in the high steeples calling
up to heaven the evidence
of sin on earth. not many
question the imploring
rusty bells paid for by the
white men and women
living in shuttered houses
and separated from the hands
up, don't shoot and crucified
people that always hear the
dirty ringing in their dreadful
days.

Flesh

I ask you to make
sense of the tangled
political mess called
my country that was
never utopian yet eager
to live into an imaginary
world glossy with color.
tell me how do you keep a
cool face about the odd
narrowing of life, hold
back tears in these white
days, keep your beating
heart from bursting from
one more politician's lie
and find time to get on
your knees, when all that
the good Lord whispers
in your ear is fainter than
the anguished cries coming
from the sinister lynching
trees? I ask you in the name
of your fatigue dressed, short
haired and blue-eyed Christ
what do you mean by God
Bless America? you see,

my aching heart would like
to know so I can explain it
tonight to my dark-skinned
crucified brother who taught
me a few things about a God
who crosses borders for the
sake of breathing life into
precious Black and Brown
human beings.

Sleepless

I suppose there is no use
telling you sleep tonight
will not make its typical
rounds. I walked to the
window where rustling
leaves from a fractured
tree branch is made to
brush against dusty glass
by a soft wind. I calculate
the darkness by turning a
light on in my study where
hours are spent awake with
thoughts while the world is
outside hanging on to other
things. perhaps, this will be
the night when I will believe
in miracles offered by the
simple sight of lovers tenderly
holding hands on the cracked
sidewalk, the dog off its leash
running wildly and shouting
its own magical line of words,
or the ghost of you with long
black wind-blown hair back
to share a warm smile with

the staggering block. I could write a simple letter to say the air is fragrant and warm with the merciful time to come and the faint sound of laughter is drawing near but I prefer not to be troubled right now with confessions—I do hope you understand!

The Jordan River

I see the world march
demanding a reckoning,
faces awakened from a
deep sleep, dark mouths
shouting at the deaf in
high places and those
hiding in the shadows
with white nationalist
dreams. I see a strip of
light breaking on walls
that must fall, on flesh
that will not rest until
injustice halts, in dark
eyes that have been to
the mountain tops and
on the faces of God's
Black children who move
nations closer to truth. I
see well enough to know
the triumph of a new world
beginning, the citizens of
earth translating Black and
Brown lives into names
that matter. I see the dusty
remains of the innocent who

were slain, Jesus raising them
from the dead to live in an
undivided house. yes, I see
the banks of the Jordan River
where captives wept for
freedom before they went
across.

The Swim

we made a beach down by the
East River from fifty-pound
sand bags and with the rebellious
delights of summer hung out until
nightfall in two languages older
than New York City. we jumped
from a train bridge into the dark
water from where old turtles came
up for air staring at us with black
eyes and swam with everything
we knew to the shoreline where
minnows gathered to applaud.
we laid silent on towels like flat
stones branded with stillness and
experienced time like a good brujo
spell. the East River moved across
the city before gangs, dope parlors,
broken homes and graves filled
with relatives and friends existed.
still, I dare say the joy from this
imaginary beach will forever cling
to our Puerto Rican hearts!

The Raffle

I bought a raffle ticket
from the church that
starts without us and
offers bread hard like
stone. drove by houses
with custom made signs
telling us in the world
we are not alone. what
I do know is there is no
use in sounding pretty
with words that never
quench thirst, food too
old to eat and eyes that
never cry about all the
moaning and suffering
going on right now on
the underside of the city
and the southern part of
the earth. how odd having
to dress up to find welcome
in the house of an English
only God and sit with people
whose eyes can't see the
Crucified One in poor flesh
and then hear them say nice

of you to come with a tone
really saying, "Spic you're in
the wrong place." I don't think
this raffle ticket will win a damn
thing but now that I have it
let me ask you Black Christ
what cross other than the Lilly
white church would you like
me to bear?

Floyd

unarmed Black men and
boys shot by the cops are
human beings with names
no longer living. I weep
dry tears hollering what
God can be thanked for the
violence of these badged
white men who unhooded
lynch? who stands against
knees on Black necks, kicks
in the back and these bullets
that bring destruction to so
many taken from us and
leaving us to rage? I cannot
understand why the good
Lord has not stopped these
uniformed offenders who believe
our lives do not matter! there
is no time for silence when
Black lives are laid out cold,
justice is bent and hate can
find rest in the world where
freedom is undone.

Riot

a city is in smoke
and the noise of civil
strife blasts the streets
with the blackness of
a just loving God. the
fire next time has taken
over urban space now
in the name of a Black
man who pleaded for air
while a white cop kneeled
on his neck. the lunatic
in the White House who
cannot weep tweeted his
presidential solution: break
the protestors' heads with
batons and shoot looters
dead. a city is ablaze for
the single Black life the
cops brazenly lynched and
not a single piece of broken
property can equal his single
human life. the riots make it
clear the brand name man who
orders murder can never write

a tweet to mask the truth that

sets us free.

Fire

I walked into the church with
an aching heart for every Black
young man who can't breathe.
I went to complain about the
places God made just wrong,
this hateful world and how
kindness is not currency for the
big White House made by slaves
with evil clouds floating over it
and waves of hollering about
injustice never making it over
two miles of fence. I looked at
the candles burning on an altar
unable to escape the hideous thought
that nothing has changed for Black and
Brown lives consumed by the rotted
dream of equality, the cracking
whip and lynching trees. after leaving
the sanctuary unknown to the Holy
Ghost, I looked down the street and
saw the battered body of Christ rising
from a bloody pool to take us by the
hand all the way to a promised land
despite my near broken faith!

Despair

I dusted the sorrow
kept on a shelf when
you went out the door
for a run and stopped
in the store that cried
wolf. then, once more
I fell to my knees when
the news of your lifeless
body stumbled to us.
I heard that singing in
a church are we yet
alive and wanted to say
we are serving a life
sentence until white
executioners are ready
to kill. for you see in
our mutilated world the
guilty almost always go
free, they are celebrated
by symphonies, praised
by presidents and prayed
for to a God who wants
them to feed on hate. we
are speechless about Black
lives gone and not a page

will be added to the White
history books anytime in
the new year!

Detention

last night a Salvadoran
child prayed in a wire
box for her freedom.
others cried, the guards
shouted silence and she
let loose a squall of tears
for the tiny brown girl
who laid next to her they
finally carried away to be
shipped back South in a plain
box. you could hear her talking
to God in the dark on tiny knees
asking heaven above to keep the
sight of her brown skin away
from the white hands throwing
American flag painted stones. I
took her hand and said with misty
eyes on one visit child the color of
your skin is beautiful like the earth
and full of brilliant life.

Sit with Me

let's sit down for a little
while at least six feet apart
in what is left of the day's
vanishing light, here on the
park bench where friends and
lovers have for years weaved
stories together without clear
beginnings or ends. let's find
ways to whisper across this
distance what we miss about
routine life, the times of dangerous
excitement, moments of everlasting
joy and even the periods curved
by a sadness that held us still in
the dark. let's look at the lights
starting to show in the windows
of buildings in the devastated
city, listen with a smile to the
singer standing on a fire escape
casting her voice the length of
the city to cheer the pandemic
faces and carry them away from
their blues. let's talk a little bit
about paradise still mysteriously
leaking light, calling into question

the degenerate god invoked by
the callous rich in a time of illness
and give daily birth to ourselves in
the knowledge that better times
are getting closer to us.

Central Park

in the neighborhood the park had
more names given to it than read
on signs at the southern entrance
closest to the lake. on any weekend
you hear children's voices rising
perfectly above the rooftops where
too picnic baskets are spread on old
blankets by tenement lovers fond of
an early evening space to empty their
hearts. on a few isolated paths at the
hilly north end of Central Park you
can walk quietly into the arms of an
afternoon stumbling with delightful
surprise on flowering stones, or see
birds on tree branches singing in
ways that drift right through you. at
night, the moon bursts with light
over the treetops whose leaves are
rattled by gentle breezes and you
swear it is whispering words too
beautiful for ordinary ears.

The Bedside

I heard the air sigh for
the first time today, felt
the earth circling space,
saw an old couple sitting
in silence, witnessed a few
kids painting their relief with
chalk on the sidewalk and
felt certain even now life is so
dear. there at the end of the
street where cars have been
parked for days it was easy to
feel the end of an era reached
and see the world as a photo
fading with change. I will not
weep for the days are still too
remarkable. I will allow the silence
of the stones almost ready to speak
to reach me. I will stand here in front
of the old woman's gasping bed for
a while longer listening to her gossip
about life already finding complete
renewal.

Juan Crow

we live on the Juan Crow
side of town where Black
Maria sent from heaven has
an apartment where she sings
nights to an infant in a second
hand bought crib. on this side
of the city Black and Brown sit
side by side on the stoops, in
the schools, the crosstown bus,
the storefront church and all the
places avoided by people with
white looks. we live on the side
of town that has what are called
inassimilable aliens who are the
people that endured far too many
years of racial violence to build a
white nation. we live with those who
recall family and friends hanging
by a rope from a tree. we live in a
world that believes a dark-skinned
Christ who was nailed to cross
judges white hate to hell. we live
in a Juan Crow world, the pretty
white churches can't see?

Spiritual

you dear brother
are gone into a
world of silence
and here we hold
your hand. on the
urban streets, we
remember you, in
churches where
protesters gather
to say their too late
prayers, we grieve
and promise not to
stop fighting for
justice and your
God given right
to live. you dear
brother imperil
the brutal cops,
revolting politicians
and the racist white
world with your
resurrection in us
and we will tell the
children the truth
today and in for

years to come. we
will say this loud in
murderous worlds, to
hate craving citizens
and the blood spilling
cops: we ain't dead and
you will never stop heaven
from making its sacred
rounds on earth.

What Matters

if I don't wake up
tomorrow let my
voice be carried
loudly in the wind
until it rests with the
cries of the poor, the
suffering, the ill, the
hungry, the homeless,
the imprisoned and
every child's tears on
the perfectly adorned
altars of the locked up
church. when I fade into
the memory of history,
with my Spanish name
dissolved by the nation
that always called me a
spic, let Angels carry
what remains of me in
dust to the place where
the lights are never out,
where Black is always
beautiful and Brown is
forever the color of God's
own magnificently jeweled

crown. if I die in this very
troubled season, with the
candles on my altar thinly
burning, the Chinese made
clocks flawlessly keeping
time, do not weep for me
but stand patiently while
you breathe in defense of
those hated, vulnerable and
weak.

Together

when a little boy in the
Spanglish world of Bronx
workers, among kids that
would never go to Harvard,
almost every night I walked
tired feet in fake Converse
sneakers to Southern Boulevard
to hear the music of Johnny
Pacheco that was played by
an outdoor speaker at a record
shop owned by a Jewish salsa
lover. man, I felt alive on that
strip imagining one day the same
kind of magical flute would be
played by my Puerto Rican lips
and bastard boys on the block
would swing their priceless souls
back and forth until the stars in
heaven turned off. the tunes from
that record shop can still make me
break a fever when I hear the
trombones, trumpets, congas,
cowbells, strings, pianos, timbales,

and dizzying lyricists conjure the
harmonies that leave you fully
woke!

Another Country

I spend days with the people
in the barrio who save me daily
with the hope they believe came
into the world. I read the Spanish
papers with stories about lunatics
and photographs of trouble in too
many places and tremble until I
hear the sweet laughter of children
and the sounds of Spanglish bubbling
from their tongues. in the morning, I
eavesdrop on the voices of men and
women talking about their lives in
another country, the family spirits that
share their residences and the things
making them stumble in an unwelcoming
nation. I have spent many hours in church
hearing ministers babble messages going
nowhere and with my people unable yet
to speak English I look for extravagant
justice and forgiving peace.

The Klan

the whole world has a
chance to see America
still lets the Klan march
the streets with their grand
imperial wizards heading
the parades and none of it
a fictional movie scene, you
see. they may not be beating
us with clubs on this side of
the Dixie line but not one
of these white ghosts with
permits to take the streets
needs a baton to make colored
people like me from inside
bleed! thankfully the Lord has
just the place to burn them up
eternally!

The Letter

Dear Rudy, I thought
you might want to look
over my shoulder from
heaven to read a few
lines. You probably
saw me reading your
favorite Psalm that
says the Lord is your
salvation and you have
nothing to fear. when
loathsome politicians
laughed about sending
anonymous agents to
batter mothers and vets
like your half brother
and father on Portland
streets. this Bible text I
put on your headstone
came into my heart. Tell
me, did you put it there
to say no matter how the
wicked advance they will
fail? despite the running
years, I can't report that
people down here are any

closer to salvation, more
like splinters are coming
out of their pores speaking
dirty English and filling
heads with white lies. on
top of all the hate, we are
in a pandemic and people
in the old neighborhood
are undertaking a journey
to meet you faster than the
priests can make it to them
to offer last rites. I am sure
you heard me calling out
for aid and wondering like
Baldwin's Staggerlee how
long will good people keep
up the freedom charade? tell
me, don't these assholes in
white robes and those submissively
watching crosses burn know by
any means necessary we shall
breathe!

Spanish Harlem

the latest beautifully Brown
people who know about planting
and picking long days in hot
fields just moved into Spanish
Harlem. they have come to the
city that promises to leave them
no less hungry for days on end
while they chew on peasant bread
that looks no more than a pancake
to the ignorant of their ways. they
use to harvest coffee on mountains
filling baskets with the high yields
that shortened their lives to make
others rich but now they labor in the
city where the good people in church
never learn their names and their days
are paid for by the cheap hour defined
by mopping floors, washing dishes,
swapping rubbish bags, building pretty
things and being maids in the U.S.A.
saying yes sir and no ma'am. with Spanish
tongues mixed with Indian words I hear
them say someday freedom will get paroled
so it can to come live with people like us
right here!

Judgement Day

God, the truth is I looked
for you all over the church, in
the candles burning on the altar,
the holy book on the pulpit, the
lips uttering in the long hour of
prayer, in the preacher's words
vacuously walking the earth, in
collection plates filled to keep a
congregation busy, in the sweet hour
of Sunday worship but I never did
find you looking for people who
weep exhausted tears or say anything
of new life to come. God, on judgment
day forgive us for looking for you in
the wrong places and not hearing you
in the screams in the jails, the migrants
singing alleluia, the children in barrios
gathered by the merciful arms of your
Angels and in the desperate you made
with love

The Name

the man in the White House
living off taxes carries his fat
belly across the links while
the country he was sworn to
serve makes the frailty of its
health the subject of a fresh
public grief. this man who
hasn't worked a day in life,
was never punished for his
crimes and utters from the
hole in his soul denials and
filthy lies cannot be more
deserving today of Judas'
fate!

Sickness

we are desperate in the
tired hours of hushed
days, waiting for truth
to speak like priests at
their altars and political
leaders to confess they
are quite fit to address the
darkness on the other side
of the door. in the ghastly
hours, doctors offer us no
cure, churches are empty,
Saints are socially distant
and God is entirely hard
of hearing. unable to stop
shivering the world waits
for someone to say never
mind the funeral flowers
and cancel the hearse the
season of illness is done
so, go on and step out of
the cursed flat light.

Illness

illness is a sneaky thing
moving in the air breathed,
resting on the surfaces of
regular things and much like
a god who never talks and
germs that the naked eye
cannot see. we wonder in
this time of social distance
about yesterday's ordinary
things that were always taken
for granted. we recall moments
when heads turned with storybook
laughter in so many places that are
now missed. the hours have never
moved this slowly and the end of
it all is not clearly seen, yet we
wait for it to come thundering louder
than this storm and dressed for a
new beginning.

Words

imagine me whispering in
your ear after sunset these
three kids and mother slipped
across the border softly talking
in a language despised on this
side of the fictive line between
two countries, unchained for the
first time in their lives, recalling
the homily of the young priest who
left his home in Brussels to sing
Spanish hymns in a land named
after a middle-eastern savior and
hiding in the shadows from agents
in helicopters who cannot see the
poor family that is the color of the
earth. pretend for just a few hours
this mother with children in flight
has arrived in the city with Brown
faces terrified of the very things you
most fear and determined to move in
in the direction of the same light you
love. let me share with you stories of
the ugliness they fled, the fear deep

in their bones and the English tongues
lashing them on Main Street America.
imagine, it's never too late to hear the
words of the trampled.

The Masquerade

looking at the world from the
edge of Main Street USA leaves
me with the nagging suspicion
when the church bells begin to
ring old-fashioned Dixieland
delights a big pinch of racial
hate masquerades as spirituality.
I keep waiting to see the lights
grow bright in churches the moment
finely dressed and highly educated
white preachers read the Word in the
scriptures that say in plain translation
of the Hebrew text liberation ended
slavery. you know, the stars God
made above the streets and shining down
on the monuments of poverty called
slums hear Black mothers' lullabies
and Brown kids' dreams but before I
forget, dear Dixieland bigots and all
you folk in the we don't want your
kind in church, when you arrive at
the heavenly gate don't be surprised
to find it shut to keep out your sick
piety and shitty-ass jive!

Wailing Wall

what do you say about the
great words discussed from
morning into the late day in
schools, churches and even
in the pubs like justice, freedom,
mercy, beauty, truth and heaven
sent love? have you noticed them
these days condemned? are they
good enough to carry in your heart?
let me raise a very different question
with you, what do you think about
talk that says Jerusalem is God's city?
my mother told me San Juan and New
York were God's cities though they
were never referenced in the good
book and when I went looking for
answers in a church the widows said
the streets that bleed are Holy! tell me
have you visited the wailing Wall on
the border, touched it, said prayers by
it for the people it keeps out? I urge
you to do it before you next think of
lofty words and have the nerve to call
upon God in English!

Evicted

we made it to the
banks of the river
with no tears for
weeping. there was
no waiting boat to
ferry us to the other
shore. we skipped
dreams across the
water though better
days will not come
God knows this year
or next!

Heaven

heaven is a long walk
away from the cutting
English of these streets.
everywhere happiness
yields sweet campesino
dreams. admission to
extravagant dinners are
free and God speaks words
that cannot be misplaced.
heaven is a ride in boundless
space where laughter spreads
like gossip and every voice
is lifted with life that sings
for spying stars. heaven is
the place where stones can
speak!

América

I am America before
spoken English and
far from any dreams.
I was here fifty years
before your Pilgrims
and with the Timucuan
had a first thanksgiving
feast. I am Brown America
with thousands of Spanish
words that named villages,
cities, mountains, rivers
and streams before you
said the earth and God at
the end of the day belongs
to no one other than you.
I am America made from the
darkest ancient clay that
you despise with children
ripped by border agents from
their mothers' arms. I am
America's aching heart, the
exile you nail to the cross
and God's thief at Golgotha
hanging on the tree to give
the world life.

Bread

I rarely thought a life
molded from clay and
destined for dust could
in the shortening years
keep hope, struggle and
dreams closer than this
festive day. today, my
heart shouts the names
of the people stumbling
to find the land that said
equality and freedom will
never be complete without
them. today, I will take the
hands of family and friends
who have touched bruises,
feel God's wind on my face
and give thanks for the souls
who taught me how to share
bread.

The Birthday

one by one, sometimes in
a bunch, the deeply sheltered
memories request a hearing
mostly in the middle of the
night when it is quiet. when
they come, I read them like
an injured book with torn pages
and let their images put a smile
on my face. just last week I
unfolded an old paper map
from a box that was full of
wrinkles and imagined the
places on it that held my life
firmly in their arms. I stared
at the names on the creased
sheet and swore each place
was singing my joys and aches
just to tell the story of the years
that broadened me. I can tell you
we all know aging better than
the unexpected farewell to loved
ones and memories good or sad
fill us with all the delicious signs
of life.

Sing

I heard it a long time
ago on the steps of the
a stoop in the prettiest
slum that trouble don't
last always and you got
to keep on, so I told myself
turn the next corner and hold
on.

The Zoo Day

we walked the four longest
blocks to the zoo entrance
and trail bikes zoomed by
with the tiniest kids riding
with helmets weighing more
than them in seats above the
back wheel of jovial riders'
bikes. we could see drifting
in the sky above the trees in
the park balloons floating with
long ribbon tails escaping into
the distance. there were so many
carried away by the wind that
we wondered whether or not they
were released with the Perez family
name inside on the bet they would
drift across the ocean and all the
way to Puerto Rico with a message
of joy from them. we looked at
each other before speaking out
loud in pedigree Spanglish from
the South Bronx to say mala suerte
que we did not send a balloon into
the air with a picture of God by
a busy water fountain making ice

cones with tropical syrup for kids
who have never seen free public
school lunch boxes with rice and
beans nor sugar cane treats.

Breathe

it was a busy year with
little time to pause by a
deep well like a sage to
breathe. now, hushed
days show us where
to find tranquility. we
spent too many weeks
not offering answers
and in this storm, they
find ways to stitch for
themselves a place in
our flesh. no one ever
thought silence had so
much to say or give to
those open to company
from within. when the
storm ends we will not
want the stillness found
too distant and we will
wish to hold it near like
a lamp in the dark.

Be Still

the evening falls and
I imagine silence after
a day taken up by sundry
judgements about a tempest
wearing us thin. I can almost
see people acting now like
Saints wherever they are
sheltered and hear prayers
said across the street against
the menace that is making
us confess how little more
than nature is flesh, bones
and blood. I pray for those
who have departed to distant
heaven from these sick parts
and wait for our speechless
God to say something about
human beings feeling in this
great divine creation steadily
undone. the night is around
me now like your shapeless
face and with the moaning
wind comes peace to offer
me bread, the cross in the
moonlight and a rest from

fatigue. I cannot say when night will come again so gently but when that time arrives doubt will not keep me from confessing your Holy presence was in the cracked hours of wounded days.

Pandemic

little birds singing
Spring for us you
carry beauty in the
world, today. little
birds without a care
sitting on branches
of tall trees sing to
us and wish us well
to make it through
today.

Imprisoned

Nelly, I have known your
dark eyes looking through
the loathsome wire fences
on the border where they
cry. in the crowded yards
where young women kick
crumbled rocks you talk to
jailers about your kids and
whisper prayers for strength
to bear the hardship. Nelly, I
have a letter for you that came
across a thousand Spanish
speaking mountains with kind
words I know are waiting to spill
out. you will no doubt read of
others who marched north, some
picked up by ICE raids in the
Good Housekeeping cities
you always dreamed, children
in the village uniformed for
school and mangoes swinging
above elderly heads. Nelly,
when you waved goodbye
beneath the immensely dark
sky and said you cannot find

sleep I wept and confessed
blessed are you Nelly among
women!

Mojado U.S.A.

this winter in the woods
on the brown dirt path
a grey bobcat roamed in
tall moist grass left by a
night rain that invited the
human inside my breast
to beat quicker than any
running steps. in all
my days of roaming on
city streets and even the
long periods of hard work
in white men's factories,
I had never seen a creature
more beautiful. I picked
up that moment that held
me in its arms and took it
with me to the banks of the
Rio Grande where my father
one day swam into a future
he could see with his dirt
colored body drenched and
dripping for years on me.
quietly, on that river shore
I whispered to the wind my
river crossing did not leave

me drenched and was not
made hiding in a rickety old
car trunk but in the schools,
the rides in buses, from east
to west and every day polished
boots with big white feet kicked
me with pink lips shouting born
here but never home, spic!

Strange

in the politics of an ignorant
age politicians are no more
certain of their steps than the
blind leading the blind into
a room. this year, by the end
of Holy Week hearts may be
no more than stones in a world
that faintly hints resurrection.
in closed churches where they
talk about miracles and Christ
returning those taken from the
world by a pandemic will not
be coming back. so now, we
are left like beggars without
bread, the desperate without
homes, an audience for Angels'
howls and bystanders who yell
at a deranged president truth
and God are dead!

Tomorrow

I want you to play the music
that calmed streets when
we saw the blood-stained
writing of kids on walls
and lamented. engulf me
with the scent of the little
village with the huge Ceiba
tree where old women roast
cashews and then sell them
in exchange for life. in the
middle of a most troubling
time let me hear voices that
sing, the clouds laughing all
night and people shouting on
rooftops and in the public squares
that they will make it to a promised
land. tonight, let me find a
thousand ways to say eternity
may one day claim us but not
today, this week, next month,
the new year nor before God
enters our hellish world dispensing
magnificent measures of hope
and peace.

Say

I,
never
save
the
lying
words
slipping
out
of his
lips.
I,
wait
for
truth
to
round
corners
wet like
dew
on
the
Spring
grass
where

dark-skinned
kids
yelling
Spanish
play
football
with a
really
round
ball.
I,
like
to roam
streets
at
night
in
search
of
God
displeased
with
him.

Social Distance

in the worst hour of Spring
just when everyone thought
themselves sturdy for simple
warmth in bright sunny days
the world was brought to its
knees by illness caused by a
tiny unseen pathogen. now,
retreating to social isolation
many begin to wonder about
temporal improvement, the
day the unkind imagination
of nature will change, closed
restaurants, cinemas, gyms,
theaters, concert halls, churches,
temples, mosques, sports arenas,
schools and the mom and pop
shops. now, alone and grabbing
any sign of light, questioning how
to dance in a time of detachment,
restricted by walls, rules and fear
whenever a neighbor coughs, missing
those dinners with friends at the local
spot, hearing every song that floats in
the air in a melancholy tone,
forming a line to reach the

grocery shelves, and praying to
believe in better days, in this
time of sorrow, we wait for life
to renew itself and the world
again to breathe free.

The Band

Tito came from
the big avenue
church carrying a
wafer in his pocket
and a quart of beer
in a brown paper bag
in his right hand. In
this desperate season
of illness when hanging
on the stoop is rare, the
city was for him still not
a lonely wilderness with
a slim chance for joy!

Forty-Five

the cameras come
on, the characters
gather, the doctors
in unison whisper
millions on earth will
suffer, thousands will
die from a new major
disease, while a clueless
head of a frightened
State poses to boast,
lie and deny the devil
in the details. the failing
president desperate for
attention, a man clearly
in cognitive decline, an
unfit leader never called
to account, the starter of
fires with absurd words,
the child of America with
a dark heart is an insane
donor of messages expected
by the public to have honest
importance but nothing useful
gets said. Behold, we cry on the
city streets, the desolate shores,

the abandoned parks, the rural
roads, the lonely hillsides and
places where heaven is mocked
by the malignant fool!

Heart

we count days
in long numbers
now, waiting for
the return of the
world we thought
lasts forever, for
voices in school
yards to once again
sound, to see in dark
eyes plenty of bright
light, and to find a
way back. today, we
weep for the dead,
pray for all flesh and
ring merciful church
bells to find strength
again to love, hope
and revive precious
dreams. today, we
lift the voices of this
whole earth, favorite
names along with the
unknown just to remind

ourselves soon and very
soon the bitter bread will
sweeten!

The Torn Veil

time will change,
the days will soften
with the laughter of
old men and women
holding hands on the
park benches and the
fractured hearts will
not forget but mend.
time will change, the
exhausted world will
make new memories
of bliss, there will be
no one to call a fool
for believing, faces
will not be covered,
touching prohibited,
and wandering light
will return. time will
change, the flowers
will blossom, rabbits
will run into the night
faster than our ticking
clocks, the birds will
sing lullabies for us to
hear and children will

laugh riotously again
in every tongue.

Dismissed

on this street where
the desperate live the
nightly news takes a
detour and the poor
that adore each other
are never rescued by
the care in this white
world given to others.
on this street dusted by
Spanish speaking grief,
the wound dressers in a
time of illness have not
come into the darkness,
journalist find thousands
of reasons to dodge this
world of tears and even
prayers from the pretty
steeple churches have gone
silent. in the bitter days
dying on this forgotten
spot the poor, the rejected
and the offended who still
learn how to speak English
tell each other at the end of

each day nobody anywhere
on earth cares a damn about
us.

Joy

there is something
tumbling in our souls,
refining its presence
in our depths, tearing
down dividing walls
of separation, relieving
us of empire's chains
and filling them with
truth that matters for
dangerous times. there
is something about the
silence on city streets,
noisy days remembered,
the kids' shadows on the
crowded playground parks
and hands held to cross
the big avenue that speak
to us still of life to come.
there is something today
that is beautiful when it
offers us the simplicity
of an empty tomb.

Ghost Town

how strangely silent is
the block tonight, the
young lovers have not
gone by holding hands
for weeks, at a distance
the church bells ring that
someone is there, and the
cloudless sky says too little
about a fair-weather spring.
how strange not to dream
into a night full of the sweet
fragrance of a new season
with crowds sharing fresh
laughter on the sidewalks.
tonight, I weep with the
generations on earth that
never thought social distance
would ever be so close to the
shivering flesh from which
meaning always flowed.

Malefactor

you never mention
the poor by name and
the barbarous filthy
rich who complain of
the noxious needy have
names you are capable
of rattling even in your
sleep. Heavens! you talk
just like someone who
stumped a toe in the open
end shoes you know were
sewn by a child slave on
the other side of the world
and across the border. and
so, there you go today on
the Avenue of the Americas
nicely dressed and tongue
tied!

The Empty Lot

I said there was a building
on the empty lot that used
to be home for me and lots
of my Spanglish speaking
people. the white landlord
who never cared to know a
thing about renters he called
spics sent an arson one night
to burn it to down and blame
it on the Brown kids. one fine
Sunday in a white church with
two pastors in suits and shoes
more expensive than mother
could ever hope to earn in a
year, I declared being happy
in the old apartment where
a good God in heaven first
said to me don't be afraid.
you know, we use to run
up and down the stairs,
fly kites on the roof, never
play cowboys and Indians,
and ran like migrants dashing
across the border or carrying
shopping bags out of a tropical

origin plane. I often said living
in that apartment with my broken
English mother life is good and
Angels even live with us!

Heaven

heaven I don't quite
know how to tell you
is not a happier place
than the stoop up the
street where the dark
haired kids sit to listen
to the IRT whistling
on the elevated tracks
above the boulevard
where stray dogs roam.
in this short life, the
filthy steps serve like a
godly throne to dispense
justice and a miracle
or two for the drunks,
junkies and down and
out poor.

Long Days

I whistled in front of
the building for the dog
to draw back from the
middle of the block where
he played with water from
last night's rain. there was
no sociable talk to be heard
on the empty street and in
my head Barber's Adagio
for Strings came flooding
out of a window that was
slightly opened with a radio
on its sill. I recalled a day
when a little boy the piece
was broadcast on the radio
when Kennedy was slain. I
wept again for him and also
for splintered days of illness
keeping the world now quiet
by day and no longer bothering
to observe mysterious stars at
night. I see people creep in the
public spaces waiting for salvation
to end the viral apocalypse and
I fall to my knees to begin a talk

with the One who will gather us
in the dark, give life to the dead
and wipe away tears from the faces
of the frightened.

Quarantine

I've been hollering
in my head all day,
no Spanish curses
taken back for the
past several hours,
and you understand
my best intentions
are behind every
word. I opened the
door and only saw
faces hidden by masks
with creases on the
edge of their eyes
evidencing smiles
and appearing to
say what a pity.

Waiting

when mothers in the broken
city cry alone, their children
play quietly on the sidewalks,
and Gabriel's silver horn does
not blow. if you enter the hushed
apartments and walk in the barren
rooms, you will meet people that
question why in a time of sickness
god is silent and politicians toss
bag loads of deceit. you know if heaven
cracked open tomorrow and a voice
leaked a word of love in this time of
sickness that should be your cue to rush
into these ruined flats to share the good
news with the wretched of the earth!

Prayer

prayer has for long been the
habit of the church for things
good and feared, the words
calling upon the inhabitants
of heaven to plummet to the
earth, a kind of loud clanging
cymbal echoing in the world,
the poetry of worship books
searching in the utter dark
for the accomplices of God
and the sounds of the talkative
church about what can be known
about beginnings and ends.
prayer has been a thing to speak
of hunger, poverty, imprisonment,
outcasts, joblessness, and thousands
of sick human beings on earth. prayer
has been like sleep surprising us with
dreams, a simple feeling in hard times,
a blessing at a masquerade ball and a
slice of heaven for this life.

The Lesson

I have never known the
city streets to have this
degree of noiselessness
despite roaming them for
more than half a century.
today, even in the sunlight
my shadow seems afraid to
come out and the impenitent
junkies typically on the east
corner cannot be found. the
cafes are empty of whispering
lovers, friends are not tucked
in restaurants gorging themselves,
and not a single table in them hosts
families saying Christian prayers
before they eat. I will sit here with the
quiet to remember the soft warmth of
night a year ago in spring, the children
then standing at the windows, the old
widows with youthful hearts and enjoy
a splendid plunge into the memories
of that lost paradise. soon, I am certain
the world will tumble back into
place and we will once again fill

the empty places so that even a last
gasp on earth will be more like a
first breath.

The Station

when you leave the elevated
subway station at the bottom
of the stairs, where many sad
springs ago the first Spanish
speaking mothers walked, in
the dimly lit social club named
Ponce you will hear the echo
of a guitar and a faint voice
nearly out of breath sing all
is fine from the bottom of old
lungs. mothers who spent the
day way downtown washing
floors on their hands and knees
stop at the pizza shop next to the
the social club to order a pie
for kids at home and they stare
out the shop window with hope
in their eyes that can alone stop
the gods of sorrow who watch them
live poor. pause here to talk and
you will learn no one expected
to be so invisible to the world
for so many long, long years.

After Hours

shout our names across
the heavens, call us to
your ever-loving arms,
let us roam yet another
tickled night down the
streets where children
played and no one was
cheated of joy. let us
find you beneath the
silvery moon, in memories
that shadow us, in warming
love and the coming light
that is always new. keep
us unafraid of imminent
dust, the unknown secrets
of expired time, the colossal
wilderness where we now
go to weep. keep us calm
in the life you know as
long, hold us by the hand
where death will never be
and before night is done
bless us with love.

The Walls

we've been sitting here
on this stoop for many
long years, keeping all
our dreams in number
2 tan paper bags that we
got at the Perez grocery
store when they didn't
have a single crease or
stain. it's a crying shame
but it doesn't matter down
here who is president, we
go on sick, unemployed,
brutally clubbed and poor
just the same. we got use
to being faceless on the
ugly corners, anonymous
in the records of history so
carefully produced by those
whose minds are no more to
us than graves. we will not
be missed when gone but
we don't mind saying you
will never dream on earth
like us.

Stoned God-Talk

listen, no matter what
the rabid preachers say
this pandemic was not
heaven sent. no sneeze,
cough or tightness in the
chest like some confused
words a few churches like
to spit was thrown across
the earth by God as Angels
blared punitive notes on big
old trumpets. look, on every
bed where fever dances God
rests too in lonely sweat, weeps
without a night of sleep and
calls new life to hurry up for
earthly sake. recall, Christ came
into the world a slave, was
arrested, beaten, mocked, and
left on a tree for dead, then
after all the unspeakable feculence,
he returned for the sick, the healthy
and the pitiless here. therefore, do
not to make the day so dim or
think grief the object of a loss, but

believe the joy to come, the world
in love and life as promised without
threat of end.

Seed

we
crossed
the
border
to this place
that never
saw
our
flowering
trees,
heard
orchids
whisper
words
to
soft
winds,
nor
noticed
the
stars
spying
our
tears.
we

crossed

the border

to

look for

the

arms

of

the

everlasting

God

who speaks

to us

in

Spanish.

Narcissus

it was only yesterday
that we looked over
the printed news to
find more than a few
words telling a tale too
different from the one
he spun today. here in
this country about the size
of China truth is too much
telling for crooked officials'
mouths and dear Emily you
cannot hear on any day the
truth told even slant. grotesquely,
the hours move on with the
same pink lips reminding a
country on the edge of hell
of its mistake, while delivering
foul punishment mingled with
the malodorous stench of a misfit
wannabe owned by Russian friends.
despite the public record, some dare
calling the impenitent and bitter twitter
of shit a blessing. you know, he will keep

remaking history to his white delight and
claim he better than Christ can get water
from stones.

Fortune Teller

on Southern Boulevard
pressed between the Jewish
Candy store and the first Chinese
Restaurant on the block that
introduced bean sprouts to
the rice and beans crowd, a
fortune teller set up a store
front shop. the neighborhood
Catholics walked by it always
looking away and claiming with
that gesture they were not in the
mood to sin. I noticed the place
one day when winos staggered
on the street in front of it making
it easy to read the wretchedness
on the block that made us curse
each day. I walked in the dimly
lit place saw a table with four chairs
placed around it, a tall candle burned
from its center and an old lady came
from a back room offering to read
my fortune for a couple of bucks.
she promised to reveal the star of
my birth, secrets kept by the church
and my destiny from heaven. well,

I had two bucks made shining shoes
on the north corner of the street, so
off we went on a magic ride where
she declared happiness and long trips
would come for me, soon. I left
the fortune teller right quick and
went back to the street and spent
the years looking for her cheap
two-dollar words. mercy, even
now the memory of the place
gives me a weird peace—the old
woman was right!

Señora

yesterday, I did not speak of
dark things you understand,
or the long days waiting to be
called home, or the hours that
passed with nowhere to go, or
the memories of a young mother
that looked out of a bedroom
window laughing. nowadays,
I spend precious time putting
life back into your maternal
love, tending to the child that
often sat with you amused by
simple things. listen, I can see
now you held down two jobs
to barely make rent, fed us
just enough food to keep
us skinny and clothed us from
a second hand shop. dear lady,
forgiveness may not heal the
lost years but you must know
sweet lady I do love you and
the gift of life you gave to
me.

Listen

once more we are
called to listen to
the beaten whose
names are never
learned. if you are
silent while they
weep in jails where
they are slandered,
the tortured One who
long ago died on a
tree will in all the
states that yet dream
him surely make it clear
to every American on
knees in a church that
faith has nearly in this
star-spangled country
bled out. stop faltering
with the impious, attend
to the One who calls from
the cold cells, shrieking
fields, assembly lines,
dishwasher hands, grass
cutters lives, cleaning
ladies' bruises, rich family

maids, construction workers'
scars, police battered dead
and violence fleeing kids.
confess the stones scattered
on the lanes and the dust
blown by the wind to every
color blind door, obey!

Not Far

heaven is not too far
from the places you
stomp on earth. you
can hear it in the birds
that sing, feel it in the
breezes of the warming
Spring and see it all over
at play. heaven is not too
far on the other side of
the wilderness distance,
in the dark corners of
uncertain days and the
dreams that never rush
away.

Twilight

last night, I sat for a long
time on the building steps
admiring the dirty avenue
of my beautiful Spanglish
city immersed in a place
with the delicious sounds
of music composed to tell
the stories of my gorgeous
sofrito people who are never
too tired to crash into night
with laughter. you may think
it odd but alone on the steps
that gracious moment made
me feel I had already lived
more than my broken English
mother ever dreamed in your
unwelcoming America. last
night, as the streets yelled
for hours against national
insanity, God threw kindness
on me.

Insomnia

the Valencia bakery gave us
day old bread with a free stick
of butter when we walked by the
shop. the aroma that drifted out
the door submerged us in God's
own mysterious first day of creation
when the initial bite of the loaf given
to us by Ana filled yesterday's empty
stomachs. in the long summer standing
on the free lunch line outside of P.S. 20,
riding the subway to Manhattan looking
at the eyes of strangers, and waking up
in the dark, I often asked God how long
would we make memories in three rooms
dressed with Spanish speaking poverty? the
clearest and most fundamental answer that
ever came back was the same old silence
separating heaven and earth.

Meditation

if at once I sense each
breath sitting here on this
rooftop beneath the grey
clouds, without a single
thought on any one thing,
staring at church steeples
scattered over many city
streets, seeing birds move
far away slowly across the
vast sky, sighting stones
laid in fire escape flower
boxes nearing speech and
listening to my heart beating
life maybe the whole world
would find a way to echo
in it and like falling rain just
drench me.

Church

there is no clock to
punch time during
the dreadful hours
of a jobless day. at
the church that still
open's its door fumes
from city buses enter
and people kneeling
at the altar pray in two
languages and leave the
place without responses.
sometimes, the wind
blows through the dark
sanctuary like a divine
spirit no one actually takes
for real. day by day, they
show up, and after many
years these people have
easily walked the distance
from New York to Jerusalem
and back. perhaps, come Sunday
the Methodist pastor in the slick
tan suit wearing leather Florsheim
shoes will announce the name of

the street where the poor can find

Jesus.

Ask

come sit with me on
these building steps
dreaming into the
language that was not
spoken at your birth.
let's watch the morning
begin to make joyful
noises like today were
Sunday, make a list of
the places handing out
food to eat, the names
of mothers loved, the
boys that never grow
old, girls who discovered
America only wants to
be whiter than snow and
the old ladies who say they
go to church just to pray for
change. come sit with me on
the stoop academics say is
in the ghetto and let's talk
until dark night comes about
the ringing in our ear and
why they should know we
learned to read, write, pray

and love in this place we

call, home!

Hard Times

hard times for too many
leave my breaking heart
with so many tears for
our short lives. hard times
that keep coming for the
poor, the tired, prohibited
lovers and all the kids made
from aches on the sick old
earth. hard times not yet
interrupted by heaven from
above and little by little just
carrying our joys away. hard
times that we just want to
send out the door with the
saddest lines that pop into
our heads. in the weary hours,
where we yet hope and sing,
Lord send us joy and let us
stand once more on your
prettiest earth.

Silence

the silence is now so easily
seen around the empty streets,
the fading moon of a rising day,
the puddled water from a past
night of rain and in all the time
that has unfolded with so much
distance. silence follows us into
sleep each night, greets the first
light of a new day, the things that
will be left unsaid, the company
we keep on walks, at meals and
play. silence is unbelievably the
rushing wind, the heaps of dust it
tosses to our feet, hushed figures
sheltered from the sick and the
speechless stranger now firmly
thriving in us. silence hardly rises
to the heavens, resists reaching for
the light but cannot make us even
now fail to see.

Undocumented God

summer on the block
with the crooked teeth kids
out from school is a time
for play. we used coat
hangers to open fire hydrants
in the middle of the avenue
that could not wait to spring
Spanglish leaks. not a single
complaint could withstand
the riotous splashing of kids
not even the cops who came by
often to shut down the pump
though we opened them again
once they left. in the summer
months on the block doors could
not keep us in, there was no flag
pledging, no school lessons about
white heroes, and no feelings of
invisibility. summers, we only needed
our Black and Brown souls to be woke
in the company of a Spanglish loving
border crossing and undocumented
God!

Third Avenue L

the Tremont Station of the
third avenue L was removed
a long time ago though the
abandoned stop still gives
hope to people who come from
the other side of the border to
settle here. the new citizens
prefer to speak Spanglish, the
older among them their mother
tongue, while teachers in public
school chatter lessons but not in
the Queens proper English. you
will never see this barrio on a
map, historians never pull open
curtains to write about what they
observe in it, famed photographers
rarely take pictures of the cheap
clothes hanging across alleys on
rope, flowers blooming on fire
escapes, and the chance cricket on
the sidewalk singing. on this corner
of earth, where full silvery moons
chase away shadows everyone
confesses to each other God finds
a way to help.

La Bodega

here at the bodega on the
corner rice is still cheap,
beans have gone up about
fifty-cents, eggs are coming
from unemployed hens and
lies roam the neighborhood
freely after the nightly news.
the aisles in the grocery store
are full of children staring at
candy, black dressed elderly
women bagging vegetables,
young mothers in search of
Similac and young boys at
a far end of the store keeping
a healthy distance from each
other stacking cans. I strolled
around the store searching for
the ghost of García Lorca to
urge him to write a few lines
about the new lost city with its
silent cafes, bars, movie houses,
shops and broken hearts. I needed
him to cross the East River once
more and wash ashore with words

to help us in this stiffening time
and tell us what hour it ends.

The Trial

listen, you may see
me cry from the other
side to which God
forgets to write letters.
look, you may see me
sit on the wall with
wide-open eyes tossing
into the wind scraps of
paper with the words
you say to us. think, I am
trying to arouse the ghost
of freedom, justice and
equality that did not turn
out right. shout, until
hate is pushed into the
silence! now, act until
you have nothing more to
give and the cruel human
beings are exiled into the
merciless abyss.

Another Country

we've heard it said time
and again, there's a promise
coming for us on this land
of racist violence. my white
brothers and sisters who are
separated from the cruelty
and lynching dare to call
the stomping rare. somehow,
they see past the harsh graves
and the years we have been
fed bitter bread. we who look
into the unrepentant eyes of
hate, fall by the hour from
the heavy loads we bear and
stumble with chains far older
than the national flag tightly
tied to our dark feet. we are
not surprised that people who
easily hang us with rope and
spend their glad days spitting
on the balm of Gilead are so
pitiless and forgetful of the
Crucified Middle Eastern Lord

who leans into the arms of
God and lives in a country
without hate.

Sunday

on the edge of the roof a
robed Angel sits pointing
a finger at East River fishing
boats that have been docked
for weeks. leaning forward
the heavenly round faced
immortal listens to two old
women on the stoop talking
about the flaws in God's world.
on concrete sidewalks neighborhood
kids with deep wishes start games
and laugh at the final curfew
hours. the flowers in city parks
will undeniably bloom differently
this year though their heavy scents
will reach us to ease the time of
sliding days. before too long, no
one will sit on the steps to cry
about this fumbled creation, instead
they will joke about the signs of
divine imperfection and let the
sun caress their flesh.

Waiting

in the tearful
time
of this
restless
season,
the world
goes on
hellishly
eager
to
choke justice.
every night
the
misplaced
hours
witness
the
notebooks
of the
damned
filled
with the
latest
story of

the
miscarriages
of
love.
I am a
witness
to people
sick
of heart,
to the lofty
things
spoken
in the
houses
of God
that end
changing
little.
I am a
witness
to the
mystic
waiting
for
God
to get
up
from
the
heavenly

throne
and
make
us
equal
and
free!

Lights Out

the lights went out
at the White House
that long ago was
built by the labor
of immigrants and
Black slaves. odd,
how quiet it seemed
with fires burning
outside. strange to
see the place lose
its way in darkness
with the rest of the
world riotously on
fire and woke. in
the weary faces
weeping protesters
begged all night
for justice to wrap
her arms around
them and gather
up hope from the
cracked hearts to
make it flow like a
righteous stream

and repair the hurt
and broken.

The Marchers

the great mass of bodies
march in the saddest hours
of Spring and the mourning
in their hearts time will not
soon overcome. they march
in defense of the beaten, shot
and killed by racists who kick,
beat and scream. the great
mass of bodies march in the
name of dreams and all the
Black men with bloodied
heads. they march to end
terror packed days, to hear the
sound of breaking chains
and whiteness made a thing
that cannot hate or leave us
America's gift wrapped
dead!

Mercy

I like sitting on the stoop
in the morning shade with
children who are held
in the mercy of God and
with them pretend to toss
words across the sky to
part the stormy clouds
and feel the warmth of
the centuries-old sun. I
love to endlessly talk with
them about words like liberty,
equality and life on earth
not sad. I cannot imagine
better things to do than
smile with Brown mothers
looking to fulfill dreams
and sing with Black fathers
hardened with pitiless years
of work the freedom songs
we create when white curses
come our way. we all like to
sit on the old steps that have
a knack for listening to the
sound of mercy declared by

the Prince of Peace who set
us free.

The Wind

we have never seen the
wind making its way across
the land, hiding in trees where
leaves whisper, teasing us by
gently exciting the pedals of
flowers, blowing out sad candles
in a lover's heart and embracing
us with a touch too often easily
unnoticed. we have never seen
the wind puffing on our deepest
cares, carrying us to distant plains,
steppes, lakes, mountains, rivers,
oceans and the foreign language
lands. today, when the wind softly
brushes our face lets whisper some
delicate words to it.

Confession

on Sunday the well-dressed
preacher tells us to repent
our sins and the restless kids
in the pews get a vague look
on their faces, while the pretty
dressed adult folk raise their hands
high like something was about
to touch them. the choir softly
sings over his shoulder like the
voices were calling on heaven
to hear every admission and step
into the flat world. we sing hymns
older than the ages of the eight
people living in my apartment put
together and they don't even speak
a word of Spanish. we've climbed
into that service for generations
but face the same vertigo when
it comes to an end. who knows,
the pretty stained-glass windows so
alien to Jesus may be nearer to God
than the city mayor who never visits
these parts.

The Funeral

the people with loving
hearts imagine your journey
to heaven. we heard precious
stories of your life, heard the
sad songs that come for us
in death, saw the family you
loved, cursed the shameful
smallness of hate, prayed
with the world driven to
march by your very last
breath and saw you push
gaily into resurrection. in
the world, time will never
be the same now that you
along with so many others
are gone, dreams for many
of us around here will not
not be all they seem, yet no
one is afraid, grief will never
swallow us up, and all the
grim actors unmasked will
write their names on dirt
and they will be brushed
away by God's own last
breath!

The Banquet

let's pull hatred into a
deep lonely grave, put
it eternally to rest,
keep it from opening
its mouth and breathing
the earth's good air. let's
make sure it will never
make others bleed. let's
chant the cause is blessed
and walk with the people
who alone will know life
in heaven.

Idolatry

over the years hundreds
have been born who have
touched my aging flesh on
bitter corners. they changed
the way my heart beats and I
keep alive a foolish hope
learned in the basement of
a Roman Catholic church
in Spanish. I squint at the
idolatry that is displayed
by churches that never see
social uprising, the history
of massacres and the daily
injustices tolerated by the
Lord's prayer people.

Halleluiah

the fair memories rise
in June's tired days, the
gentle light promising
to stay with me in the
dark, the joyful songs
loudly playing in this
injured world to scatter
hate, the recollections of
faces in doorways long
gone, the precious dreams
that bring back a childhood
made on the shoreline of a
Bronx beach full of hope
and the long talks with
friends lost along the way
on the stoops. I do believe
tears have power, they keep
us moving along in the harsh
years and help us yell halleluiah
in the places stinging arrows
cannot hurt us and where all
dreams band together until at
last they come true.

Freedom

freedom is a thing that lives in
our hearts, an item brighter than
flames from a rising fire in a
thick dry forest, an idea more
promising than hymns sung in
churches where those exploited
by the savagery of the rich pray
and a worldly item nourished in
time by the sweet dreams of the
starving poor. freedom is a thing
that counts on truth, breaks every
chain made of lies, arrives with a
great deal of pain and announces
the prophets' vision of justice with
fierce peace. freedom does not
ever leave us the same, it is not the
product of hype and was established
in the world before becoming a word
in the English dictionary or just sick
ass jive from politicians. freedom
cannot sell us, brand us, chain us, lynch
us nor tell us Custer didn't die in the name
of white sin!

Dream

I heard you had a dream
that was made illegal by
the folks proud of having
roots in the devil's own
slave trade and who love it
when dark-skinned folks'
holler and mourn. I heard
you read from a Bible nailed
to a tree by people who like
the one pieced together on
slavers' ships and written
with the blood of Indians,
Africans and Mexicans on
land renamed in pretty white
English that declares the gates
of Eden closed. I heard you
say in the sweet night the dreams
of wretched people on this great
earth are not illegal!

The Chain

I will not change my
name to have it speak
English, it will make
the same sounds that
were on my mother's
lips and not a single
police stick can beat
it out of me. I will
write on city walls a
thousand names in
Spanish until the man
from the lower region
of Galilee comes to clear
the loathing air and whisper
things to me about Ana,
María, Emilia, Miguel,
Pablo, Roberto, Carlos,
Maribel, Sonia, Ramon,
Tito, Lelo, El Sapo, Pedro
y la Nena. come Sunday,
the nationalist preachers
will not find me listening
to anything better than love
and come evening beneath
a bright moon I will shatter

with friends about kindness
and being delivered at the
hour of death to a campesino
God who never spoke a word
of hate.

Delight

in the early morning hours
when art is invented to keep
a new day company simple
words say more to us in the
spaces between them. we have
tried to write of life in books,
to brush it across canvases, to
lift it up in song and hear it
whistled from musicians own
lips. still, a blindfold to our
deepest dreams remain and the
passage to the soul is hardly
uncovered. perhaps, today we
will escape the laws of nature
and enter hidden places where
God must surely dwell.

Say It

say it loud, say it proud
say it everywhere you
go, say it Black, say it
Brown, let it rage, say
it for many lives ago,
and for those to come,
say it to the cops, the
pastors, the priests, the
politicians, the rich white
church, the president in
hooded white sheets, the
advisors in the Big House
who are all full-of-shit, say
it in the sparkling light and
Blackest night, say it to the
judges with no memory of
right and say at the grave
yard with people who no
longer breath, say it to
strangers facing hate, say
it with all the sadness of
8 minutes and 46 seconds,
say it with the mourning
that comes with each new
day, but say I do bloody care

and despite it all God is not
done with the whitest plague
of ignorance, greed, and hate
on earth and neither are we!

The Veil

the veil was ripped
from east to west,
north to south, by
shouts and screams,
the cops and secret
service, in desolate
hearts and the loath
to be silent. the veil
was torn from top to
bottom before the
arrival of Christ on
Good Friday, ragged
by the white need to
beat, stomp, and choke
the life out of Black
and Brown America
like it has for years
in Puerto Rico, El
Salvador, Honduras,
Guatemala, Central
America and Africa. the veil was
torn today by press
clips, next week by
the decent people who
never talk back, for many

more years to come by
the poverty, hate, racism,
violence, toxic politicians
and brand name church
that never could see
Christ's disfigured hands
multiplying five loaves
and two fish.

TikTok

stop the clock on the
stadium wall, have a
look at the empty seats,
let the Tulsa skies with
stars shine bright, write
it down, pass it around,
smile for a good long time,
for the TikTok teens and
K-Pop fans are the talk of
the town on all the Sunday
amen screens. come Fall,
the Big House on Black
Lives Matter Plaza with
all the flunkies who are
cursed for sharing wicked
dreams will face eviction
and a country saying don't
let the door hit you on the
way out. in the quiet passage
of time the people with border
scars, the young Black men
gasping for air, God's own
kin murdered for loving in
their own way, the elderly
who are daily more bent,

women abused, touched, beaten,
raped and the Brown boys and
girls facing sickness and death
in cages are fired up. Stand on any
corner and I'll bet you see them
rising up against the man who
hides in bunkers and pretends to
be king!

End Time

predictably the border patrol
officers make bets to pass time
on guard at US concentration
camps about how many kids
fit in a cage or wetback adults
in a single room. they spend
lots of time laughing about
young girls in soiled under
garments and women and
children sexually abused. the
word illegal is a license to shove
crap in the mouths of God's
innocent flesh. I am surprised
the president has not already
contracted a company with
taxpayer funds to develop a
camera that puts value on the
color of skin whenever pictures
are taken on American soil and
that shouts bingo when the lens
captures white. you likely heard
about Christians insisting the
latest dispensation from heaven
says the world is in its last days
so no one should worry about

what is happening on the border
for its a sign of the imminent end
but I wish the last day of the world
would hurry up and come just
for them so the men, women,
and children in the camps along
with gray-haired relatives on
the other side of the border can
finally live free!

Main Street

I
walked
down
your main
street
looking
around to take
it all in
with
these eyes
made in
the
USA
by a
generation
from
Spanish
lands.
I
saw
us
living
worlds
apart

and
watched
you
throw
stones
at us
while
your
white
friends
took
pictures
of
the
bigotry.
all I can
say
is
surprise
in the
beginning
was the
Word
and
every
dark
face
on
this
kind

earth
was in
it.

POTUS

in a time of uncertainty
I wonder can prayers make
an absent God disturb us
to act kindly, turn away
from violence, and fall in
love with the colors of the
earth? in a country slowly
dying I wonder when will
people start pointing with
a middle finger at offending
politicians, fiercely demand
the gates of hell close and
offer aid to citizens who are
ruthlessly beaten and filling
up graves? in a culture of cruelty
is there anyone in church ready
to denounce the POTUS and his
prosperity preachers that delight
in rotted democracy? I wonder how
many sermons will be preached on
Sunday that deplore the scoundrel
in the Oval Office who eats the weak,
while holding a Bible to promote all
his villainous deeds? together, let

us weep for God who has been driven
into exile!

Dignity

you are somebody like
beauty, justice and peace.
your Black and Brown
souls were soaked in the
Creator's magnificent
being. the lies in the mouths
of men and women who only
dream a white Heaven are
oblivious to the love that
binds you from above and
has you walk with dignity
here below. when you see
the darkness grab hold of
light and let your sweet
story begin.

The Lord's Prayer

our sweet God who art in
heaven forgive my stuttering
speech and these eyes with
hesitant praise. I tell you on
scrapped knees, there are a
whole lot of people who are
not the least bit certain your
reign will come, they feel your
instruction is about as valuable
as an old dust mop and they are
convinced you will not assist
them like the stories read in
Sunday's book. did I tell you
there is a White Jesus in pretty
churches shouting praises for
Confederate flags, Generals
and monuments to slavery?
Sweet Lord, if you hear me
give us this day without racist
insanity and lead us into a
deliverance like you did for
Jesus when he got lynched on
a tree! God in heaven take our
blistered hands and tell us bitter
these days will end, soon.

Words

some words are put to use
for heavenly purposes, one
by one inviting the attentive
to be stirred, pretending to be
spoken by God's own tongue
and addressing the hardships
and all the pestilence that life
gives. in the beginning, we
found them lurking about in the
shadows, they always seemed
more complicated than simple
things suspected and not once did
a single word give us signs of
understanding a damn thing.
some words never seem to mean
what they say rolling off tongues
with imperfection, making all kinds
of sounds in open spaces, totally
oblivious to the fact that the first
and absolute reality sometimes
called God emerged from the
silence.

Escape

in black of night
on tracks without
trains people enslaved
escaped to freedom.
they paid with hope,
dreams, nerve and
blood to make it to
a new place north
to be free of chains.
Harriet said hush on
the freedom walks,
the other side is not
far and there at liberty
place every voice can
sing. in school, I read
about her joyful sounds,
Hughes lament of Jim
Crow towns, color lines,
and later the death of a
Jim Crow world where
white and colored could
not mix. things have in
some ways changed but
Lord how they do remain
the same, Black Brothers

and Sisters are killed by
cops, dumped in obscene
graves, dangled on trees
by hate and Brown people
are chained and jailed for
fleeing violence born in
the USA. you know, Harriet's
freedom train came to my old
church one day that turned
into a safe house. we ran a new
underground railroad offering
sanctuary to Brown human beings
who made border crossings to
escape slaughter, rape and the
violence dollar backed war.
today, I say we still have a train
to catch on which to lift every
voice with songs of freedom!

Song

Lord have mercy for
us now, not yesterday
nor the day that is slowly
on its way. Lord, take a
good look at the faces of
my barrio people that are
Black, Brown, Yellow,
Red and Irish White that
together haven't a single
penny of means. Lord,
have enough pity on our
spinning dreams to hold
open the gates of heaven
for us here on your good
earth.

Dig

bite your tongue
beneath the flag
until English lies
are carried out to
sea. this land long
before Jamestown
was home you see
to me.

Se Habla

tu sabe, we talk como
the words ask to play
when they jump from
our Spanglish lenguas
to spin stories full of
promesas along with
sueños no one ever put
up for sale. we sit on
stoops para levantar
opinions about the
sweet language recipe
born in a northern city
that gave birth to Black
and Brown raperos
bursting with pleas.
sabes que we speak a
sofrito English, refried
words with a taste of
órale people, the sweet
delicious chateo about
pay day, communion
wafers melting in your
mouth, the Jewish candy
store owner saying Spanish
names and Black tears

falling from our brown
faces in todos los places.
mira, we go to public school,
work all day, and pray in
church, in languages that
gather up our scattered
pieces to make Any Place
Street a sweet old home.

Divine

in my
barrio,
the blind
old man
who sits
with
friends
in front
of the
Perez
bodega
breaks
things
down
for us.
some,
expect
clear
thoughts
and
original
insights to
come
from

El Diario
but
we
had
him all
day.
el viejo
ciego,
never
cared
too much
about
the incurable
words of
the local
priest
whose
good news
never
came.
down
this way,
this old
man
was
resigned
to
tell it
like
it is

and
no
one ever
complained
about his
uncensured
tongue.

Soledad

in my country,
we weep without
end, the poor sing
for another day
to dream, dawn
arrives sadly like
it did yesterday,
and we walk into
the hours of the
working day to
end no richer. in
my country, we
see the beautiful
light, the reasons
to live and faces
with moving lips
that shout you
don't belong. in
my country, we
beg God to make
a way before the
red, white and
blue lets us fade
into a landscape
of dust.

No Ladder to Heaven

I walked down the soaked
avenue thinking it rained
enough for next week and
the water forming puddles
on the dirty sidewalk still
could not lift the tenements
to heaven. strange to admit
I have lived far from my own
country though its air fills
my lungs and every school
lesson that made so many
in the neighborhood sick is
imprinted so deeply in me that
I escape them only by admitting
the scandalous condition of my
own soul. what is happening
today in the barrio never waits
for news ink to dry with the
stories of its people that are
innocent and fresh like their
children's dreams. for many
years, I have looked for the
expert who makes bread from
stones, castes spells after storms
and doesn't require any person

to be documented to experience
life. you might like to ask me
why search? well, I read about it
in a prayer book that aimed to
disabuse faith of illusions and
assured me life is about bringing
back sweet paradise just one
more time.

Meditation

we cannot control the day
that sweeps us into it. but
there is no need to resist the
way it makes things plain.
time will keep beating its
way near and we will watch
memories arise from places
that have become transparent
in unforeseen ways. go among
the city noise, the strangeness
of an unvisited street and count
your breath until right then you
experience yourself quite in the
moment, still.

Independence Day

a hot wind blew on
Independence Day in
the time of wandering
away from faces in the
crowd. window shades
were opened for coming
nightfall and the lonely
shouts of fireworks were
lighting up the dark while
people talked until sunrise
of freedom returning to make
a home again in us. something
about this day will exhaust us
with legendary hope and make
us wonder why America is
turning away from the things
that make it grand or why
so many citizens believe a
confederate flag is a sign
of liberty?

July 4th

in the Black Hills of South
Dakota the granite cut faces
of four presidents were
carved on first nation's
land to commemorate the
first 150 years of European
history on pilfered earth. on
this day America remember
the dark hands of creation
given birth on this native
soil and hear the very first
songs of freedom, see the
trail of tears and recall with
Red souls the horrors of a
white face history.

Soon

some endings cannot come
quick enough to make dark
feelings tumble into a near
endless vacancy. we find
ways to laugh beneath the
rainy clouds and with chains
tightened to hurt and shorten
our steps. someday our ancient
scars will get a hearing in a
place beyond the stars and we
will sing glory be to the man of
color who was illegally nailed
to the tree that never could touch
executioners' hearts.

Few Words

I am not a politician being
more accustomed to sharing
thoughts in a classroom with
students who aim to work on
the failures of society from the
platform of the church. I have
no more than a minor voice in a
society that idolizes the shameful
practices of those laughing about
what pastors, prophets, nuns, and
priests have to say about the rich
galloping over the poor just to
make a buck. I have put my love
with the people who count for little,
the one's locked up at the border,
lynched in jails, on trees, the news,
in churches, schools and by the
politicians taking handouts from
stone-hearted wealthy thieves. I
have too few words left for questions
and wonder will hate find its way
back to love and when will God
hurl answers to earth?

Memories

I sit on the summer
earth awake with kind
memories of days that
still live in a different
time. I go dreaming
with them like they
were heaven sent to
drift past the places
that sometimes swell
in me with tears. at
night, your voices come
to me speaking Spanish
with the weighty sense
of home. I sit in the
place of long ago and
confess how easily my
family separated in
childhood comes to
me now.

The Pessimist

religion is a thing
explained that tells
us nothing about the
age of the earth, the
size of the moon nor
where on the other side
of stars is heaven. religion
is a thing that holds some
together like strangers
on a bus. religion, I once
heard a priest say is bones
beneath flesh, meaning for
lives and all the difficult
subjects that are pondered
by many in an unassuming
church. I say religion is more
than flowered altars with
candles aflame, the gods
that are prayed to and bent
notes singing their way up
to the clouds. I also confess
religion does little more in the
barrio than blush after spitting
up the Bible verses it eats.

Sugarcane

we chewed on a stalk
of sugarcane while the
Bronx wind whistled
across the street to the
Viejo's cart piled high
with them. on that hot
summer day, we made
a thousand journeys by
the bite to Puerto Rico
and trouble shrank for
the moment into honied
tastes. the scooters we
made from old skates,
milk boxes and pieces
of board rested on the
curve and we laughed
about blades of grass
pushing up from cracks
on the sidewalk. had
you been there, sitting
on the stoop, chewing
sugarcane with us, I bet
not a single peddler of
stories about the end of

the world would have
kept you from huddling
with us to say we were
born long before the
country we call home
happened.

The Carol

we are in the year when
the big political questions
rush out from behind the
veil and have need of good
answers. we are in a time
when dusty walls no matter
how high cannot hide feelings
of dread that border guards
with Spanish names must
even know. we are in the days
of wanting to look back on
yesterday free of the shameful
weeks with so many hours to
brutalize, silence and kill in
the name of a country that
has put liberty and equality
up for sale. we are in a time
of history that requires us not
to speak inaudibly of unholy
pious hate, partisan conceit
and the people that today and
ever since have been endlessly
betrayed. we are in the year
for our hearts to listen for the

distant church bells ringing to
call us to love.

Awake

when you recall the bruises
and think out loud about the
children selling flowers on
the big avenue do not forget
to look at the sparrows already
near. one of them is chirping,
the other is looking at you, the
street kids are smiling and the
new day will permit you to dream
in the light.

The Other Moon

the mango kids are
leaning on parked
cars tonight. they
are jumping up and
down in the silvery
moonlight, skipping
rope with their own
shadows and like a
river making noises
similar to prayer out
of church. the elderly
watch with tenderness
in their eyes while the
sparkling rush of youth
makes it way to the old
stoop where they sit. no
one bothers to count the
hours they pass together
in this hateful country
and these sweetly veined
sidewalks keep chanting
the sofrito musicals that
one day will play in the
vaguest saloons, on the

big stage and the places
that never leave anyone
alone.

Better Days

for my people who want
to live in a world that values
their dreams. for my people
who bend their knees to say
a little prayer for peace. for
my people that untangled
themselves from hate and
believe in a coming world
set free. for my people
without a penny to their
names who rub stones
to make them speak of
better times to come. I
love you with my woke
eyes!

Little Green Men

Lord,
do you still
weep
at what you
see? then,
come near
to shed a few
tears with
me.
Lord,
don't let
nightmares
come true
and
block the
politicians
keeping justice
from a good
long reach.
Lord,
do you still
bleed?
well, shed
a little bit

more for
us!

The Spell

while truth marches on
these American streets,
idles on TikTok screens
or talks mail for election
day, the orange tyrant
schemes with Senators,
spellbound citizens and
errant Christians to make
a fatuous nationalist liar
a 21st century king.

Open Eyes

you disbelieved that
God-fearing white
Christians can ever
be driven by racist
hate, then 24 mostly
Brown kids died in
detention camps,
more than 800 in
the border crossing
to America this last
year and by the wicked
hands of the white boys
and girls in blue you
say matter. you learned
to say things behind
closed doors, but it
leaked through the
cracks when you said
those damn illegal aliens,
Muslims, Black, Brown,
liberals and Queers
deserve every damn
atrocity that since the
days of the Pilgrims
got sent their way!

listen, your first president
was a slaver, another a
Black women rapist, a
third an Indian killer and
more than one a good
old friend to the KKK
and that old fashioned
piety making your big
steeple church rich and
favoring those who look
like you. yeah, you think
I am too angry for saying
your white, blond haired
and blue eyed Jesus does
not resemble the middle
eastern dark-skinned
Jew the self-righteously
pious nailed to a tree
just like your church
with the same hateful
ignorance keeps quiet
about the white inhumanity
that leaves Black and
Brown children of God
swinging from trees,
rotting in jails and paid
too little to eat. listen,
your God is a white
racist who never did
make the pages of the

Holy book save as a
figure to be drowned
in the Red Sea!

Revelation

Juneteenth in Galveston,
Texas, 1865 the revelation
day when delayed news of
freedom came with more than
babbling noise to God's Black
children enslaved. Juneteenth,
the day that is far more than
a glad shout, a time that calls
America to let freedom bells
sound for those whose blood
was spilled in the name of
white whips, chains and the
hanging trees that held terror
in one hand and the denial of
liberty in the other. Juneteenth,
the day that keeps on telling us
not to leave the world just the
way it was when we came in,
the day never mumbling inequality
always hollering for America to
be a place where no dark skinned
human being is beaten to a pool of
blood by white human beings full of
hate, viciousness and rape. Juneteenth,

declares freedom bleached the color
white is an abominable lie.

www.ingramcontent.com/pod-product-compliance
Lightning Source LLC
Chambersburg PA
CBHW060338100426
42812CB00003B/1038